With My Lips Pressed to tł

Charlotte Baldwin

Published by Nine Pens Press
2023
www.ninepens.co.uk

The right of the author to be identified as the author of this work has been asserted by them in accordance with the Copyright, Designs and Patents act 1988
ISBN: 978-1-7391517-0-6
016

With my lips pressed to the ear of the Earth

I kneel and confess.

Apology

'I am sorry, mother, but...'

1. I will use old trees to write this down
2. The roads offered speed with a side of fumes, and I said *yes*
3. Everything I ate came wrapped — like an offering — in plastic

There is no reply.

Appeasement

I tell her how since I gave up office life, the rooms in my heart
have ivy reaching around the windows, that I know this was a gift
from her and I am here, under the beech tree, to give thanks.

I tell her of the morning I stood here watching a deer surge over a
barbed wire fence in the snow —
how I forgot to move my feet.

Love

I say it aloud. *I love you.*
The soft soil beneath me
gives a little, cradles the cap
of each mushroom knee.

It's not enough. What I want to say
runs for a path through the long grass,
finds itself so wide it cannot pass
through the field-gate of my mouth.

Remorse

I speak with my hands, breaking
the pastry crust of the topsoil.
I peel out rusted ring pulls,
pack black crescents behind
each white nail. I hug
what cannot be hugged and it is sweeter
than the taste of nectar from the trumpet
of a nettle flower, and I am sorrier
than any child who ever learned, too
late, what it means to be ungrateful.

I shit a white rabbit

into my Air BnB host's toilet
and feel normal about it,
wipe the stray hairs away
and prepare to flush -
but the rabbit climbs
from the toilet and plops
onto the blue tiles
where it lays convulsing,
its fur strangely clean,
a little wet. Our eyes meet.
I imagine washing my hands,
returning to the breakfast table,
zipping my suitcase in the hall
and driving home as if nothing had happened,
then later my host collecting the sheets,
checking the en suite -
the strained politeness of her feedback:
We noticed a small furry item was left on the floor of the guest bathroom. A mop
and bucket would have been made available for your use upon request.
I pick up the rabbit. Its wet warmth
the most disgusting thing
I have ever touched, my hands
will never feel clean again
but pity kicks in - perhaps
I could take it to a sanctuary
for retired magicians' rabbits?
Staff with kind faces and airtex shirts
would clean it so it could nibble

cabbage stalks, be adopted
by a small child for an annual fee.
I almost believe in this future
for the rabbit, whose eyes have not left mine

as though it is watching the promotional video
for the sanctuary unfolding in my head -
we both almost believe it and suddenly everything
comes down to three things:
me, the rabbit, the flush handle.

I shared an ale with John Barleycorn

and neither of us were wearing shoes and the empties
leaked onto our toes while the sun hung red faced
from a tree and the dregs of the harvest stood waiting
for rains which never came and two hours earlier
I staked my last field in a poker hand I should have won
and no one but my father had ever spoken of John Barleycorn
but there he sat on the fallen tree with his tankard
so I tried to explain how we could find his song on YouTube
sing along to the tale of his triumphant drunken return
from oblivion   each harvest growing like a miracle
from his tomfoolery   tales I sung with my father who sang them
with his father but he shook his head and swigged
and the summer smelled sweet as an open wound
and John Barleycorn puffed oak smoke from his pipe
and traced the path of the old ways with a calloused finger
and I felt a fight climb from the bottom of the bottle
to join the line of things that were all my fault
and John Barleycorn saw its little balled fists
and chewed the yellow husks of his fingernails
so I punched him because he should have hated me
and all of us for what we had done to him
and I punched him because my dream of country life
lay in the yard with its throat cut and the earth's dry mouths
filling with its blood and I punched him because his world
lay buried beneath the rusting barley beside my father's

and John Barleycorn's crooked nose dripped blood
slowly into their invisible graves black as oil
and he asked me why no one knew the words of his song
anymore if we all carried it round in our pockets.

an ill wind

a coil of nothing unspools   pushes   bullying the air
        backflips   into town   grabbing hair   howling
    down the late night street   it never used to be like this
      we carry on laughing   watch as it peels   my umbrella
from its spokes   a spider   plucking a steel fly   from its
web
        it blows again   harder   slams us against brickwork
    puffs its skinless lungs   harder and harder

one by one it picks up   people we know   with invisible teeth
        chews on them   as they scream
put me down   put me down   we watch frozen
        they'll be ok   it won't drop them   on the asphalt
    we should do something   someone says   it's not too late
someone should do something   we all nod   no one moves

Families Can Only Be Grown on Arable Land

In the kitchen of the farmhouse on the farm
where the well has dried up and nothing is growing,
the family breakfast with their good dog.
"Today," announces the farmer to his wife,
"let's farm inside the house for a change."
His wife is wearing earrings and a dress
which will make farming difficult,
but the day is pressing on so they get to it, milking
their empty cups, picking photographs
from the orchard of the walls, tossing everything
into baskets full of holes. The dog
drinks what is left of the beer and falls into a river
forcing its way across the kitchen floor.

From the kitchen table the farmer's daughter
farms storybooks on scrap paper, books about birds
with no clips on their wings, who lift from the paper,
look carefully around the flooding kitchen
then escape through the open window.
A boat floats quietly along the river that has grown
between the farmer and his wife, all its windows aflame.

The zookeeper asks me if I would like to hold the scorpion

and assures me it's safe. *Very friendly*, he beams, eager as a child with
a card trick. *Special chance just for you!* His brown eyes plead with me;
a small crowd gathers. Disappointing him feels worse than being
stung, so I nod and hold out my hand, palm up. The scorpion's black
feet land sharp and weightless on my skin, needles balancing on a
magnet, so real that for a moment I forget who the zookeeper
reminds me of. *Try not to move too much*, he whispers, as its tail lashes
against my thumb.

Eco-Therapy

It's your third session with the support group and today everyone will sit in a circle in the park because nature is very healing. The grass is damp from yesterday's rain; hay fever prickles your nose. Next to you, a woman whose name you can't remember twists a ring nervously around her finger. On command, you close your eyes.

I. Guided meditation

Follow a small dirt track off the main road between trees. You assume you are supposed to walk to discover something about yourself, but the trees are too close to each other, snuffing the last reach of sky. Woods mean frightening things to you; TV murder, werewolves. Here you're a victim of the path itself, its thorns grazing your knees, branches tugging your hair. You long to turn back, but the vanishing point calls to you from its kernel of wildness and something in you answers.

The group speaks of woodland pools, cushions of moss, singing birds. You fake enthusiasm, pretend you sat by a waterfall.

II. When was the last time you interacted with the natural world?

It's been raining for fourteen days and you are on the verge of emigrating. Someone you know in very limited ways posts a picture of bone broth, labelling it #comfortfood and you decide to make your own. You crave the guilty pleasure of boiled bones, all their meat slipped off like loose clothes. The white-hatted butcher in your local supermarket smiles as she gives you her offcuts, packs into a small plastic box the bits too ugly

14

for the chiller trays; trunks of yellow bone, tangled spools of gristle. Collectively, they push your sick button, but you pretend to find them appetising as she wraps the box in white plastic and seals it with a price sticker. Later, you boil the bones with garlic, salt and thyme. They smell sweet and grassy, filling the house with the cooked ghosts of grazers. You stir with your eyes closed, knowing this broth is too real to ever eat, knowing you would be a monster to throw it away.

You tell a story about walking a friend's spaniel through fields by a railway line. You invent the place wholesale, nettles and all. Someone asks if the trains were noisy. 'Very,' you say, 'but infrequent.'

III. Remember a natural place where you felt you belonged.

You're ten years old, swimming in a river basin somewhere near Oxford, your skinny arms brown beneath your Scratch 'n' Sniff T-shirt (which no longer smells like a chocolate milkshake). It's the year before the river turns dirty and part of you wishes you had not stowed this memory so carefully, tissue papering it away with no idea what it could do to you after twenty years in flats and offices. You keep your distance from the tumble of the weir where teenagers are drinking beers and dropping from a rope, stay out where the river curves. You swim with fish and water-boatmen and for the first time do not begrudge them their place in the water, accept them as fellow swimmers though they have the wrong number of legs. This is what it feels like to belong, you think. Time balls itself around the moment, a snow globe ready for the wellness support group

to shake later, though you don't know it as you slide through the cold water.

15

This time when you open your eyes you don't lie. You are not healed by what you say any more than you are healed by the trees, the nods of the group, the curls of blossom blowing slowly across the grass. You are not healed but you have remembered something important.

Translated From the Water

You have stood a long time
with your socks off, allowing me
to laugh at you. I know

you do not speak my language.
Neither does the kingfisher,
but she hears the call to flow. You -

even if you were to dive in, or wade
with chattering teeth while my cool tongues
tasted your milky legs -

you would interrupt both of us.
If you could understand me I would share
the secret of rolling without bruises,

our name for the shiver that follows
a piercing by beak or boatman.
I could make you weightless

and sing to you of stones whose faces
I polished in thin summers,
when I had barely strength to push

through the irises. You could ask me
what I live for; I would say the sea,
the salty-jawed sea.

I could tell you our word for the thrill
of pouring away the self.
What would you translate it to?

The Obligations of Confessional Poetry

I.

A literary version of a Heat magazine exposé, confessional poetry offers dirty-linen accounts of the poet and their family. It is necessary for confessional poets to have suffered in ways more significant than getting on the wrong train or losing their keys, and because they are supposed to tell the truth they will be measured against a yardstick of elastic. They do not make pastry or read light fiction. Their houses should have leaks and at least one ghost.

II.

Confessional poets use 'I's the way some cooks use salt. They never get bored of its flavour but may hide it behind strong chilli, in the second person. Here they are being strict with themselves, whispering *I,I,I* but only under their breath, noisily pressing delete if they type *I* instead of *you*.

They remind themselves daily that the confessional is only apparently personal[1], though it must have plenty of emotional fuel running through it like paraffin in a lamp. It is difficult to tell whether this fuel is present until a lit match is held to the poem, often resulting in singed eyebrows and minor burns. Close inspection of the fingernails of confessional poets will reveal yellowed tips and a peculiar odour from testing their poems in this way.

---

[1] Disclaimer coined by Sharon Olds.

III.

Confessional poetry is not assessed by actuaries as a high-risk activity.

Newcomers brave the whiteness of their notebooks in search of truth, acknowledging the possibility of holiness while also remaining sufficiently concerned about dinner times, shoelaces and newspapers.

Believing they have control over their search, that their poems are simply a component of their varied lives - like golf or swimming which they may also enjoy - these poets are unable to recognise that truth is using them to find itself and they have taken up a hobby more dangerous than first anticipated[2]. By the time they realise the danger, it is too late to take up yoga or painting watercolours of kittens.

For these poets, the gradual alienation of family members defines their path through confessional poetry as one secret after another is offered up to the white page, trussed in the ceremonial garb of metaphor. Children and spouses may find this a particularly offensive practice, withdrawing first their secrets, then their trust. Opinions, affection and invariably their physical presence in the poet's life usually follow until eventually truth has the poet exactly where they want them: alone, with nothing to do but look for answers to strange questions they do not remember asking.

---

[2] Suicide rates are higher among poets than artists of other discipline (Wiltsey Stirman). While poetry often appears to be an appealing method of controlling unpredictable emotions, in practice poems cannot be controlled and most poets are, in fact, aggressively controlled by their unpredictable poems.

IV.

Confessional poets practice a religion they will never understand. With no wooden screen and no holy ear into which they may empty their souls, they kneel trembling before the white god of their paper, yearning for redemption. In the silence which follows each scrawl, the poet assumes they must offload yet more, an impulse which rapidly becomes a spiritual game of strip poker: the more they lay themselves bare, the more they must surely be redeemed. Only when they begin to peel off their actual skin do they realise that the paper, and beyond it the world, remain indifferent. To console themselves, confessional poets finally turn to the devil, who confusingly also appears as a sheet of white paper offering redemption. [3]

V.

The devil, once invited in, is keen to remain and become directly involved in the poet's life, inverting the glass bowl of their mind[4] and leaving them to rage quietly in it while laughing at them from the back row of book readings, or from behind their therapist's swivel chair. Their poems may begin to vaguely address this malign force but are rarely able to actually name it. Resulting poems are intoxicating to readers and addictive to their writers, who feel sure that if they can only

---

[3] In her 20s, Sharon Olds made a pact with the devil to write poetry. She admits to having done more accusing than confessing following this pact, in which she promised to give up everything she had learned in exchange for the devil's skilled assistance with her poems.

[4] In *For John, Who Begs Me Not to Enquire Further*, Anne Sexton inverted her bowl. For all its cracked stars and for all her attempts to cover it with skin as though dressing an orange, her account remains a haunting cautionary tale.

persist long enough to find the right words to name this force, they will end its jurisdiction over their lives.

VI.

The poet enters a creative night. Their every blood cell sobs with ill-spirits[5]. A passenger on the life raft of the page, they slip from the moorings of their life, out into dark waters. They row as if their life depends on it. Some are rowing towards God.[6] Some towards hope. Each word takes them closer to the bottom of the page.

VII.

The poets are frightened of the water, which squirms and licks the horizon as they edge further from the shore.

They check their pockets for the lighters once used to test their poems for emotional fuel, though emotion is a fuel they no longer burn; if they do not have a lighter, any flame will do. Candle. Hob. Oven.

VIII.

The poet[7] opens the windows in the children's bedroom, kisses them in their sleep, then seals the door with duct tape and turns on the gas. She lowers her head towards hope, who waits just beyond the gate of blue flames.

---

[5] From Robert Lowell's *Skunk Hour,* which names the experience of this advanced stage of the Confessional experience as 'one dark night' of skunks, graveyards and sour cream.

[6] *The Awful Rowing Towards God,* Anne Sexton

[7] Sylvia Plath; may she rest long in wordless peace.

Letter to a Long-Term Illness

I lived twenty lives as a sorceress before you came,
each of them more impossible than the last.
I watched rivers pick themselves up
and stroppily spill their innards
over new ground at my smallest command.
I conducted rabbit operas, choreographed
a deer ballet of improvised leaps,
tuned grasshopper orchestras
for their evening performance,
persuaded grass snakes to offer their length
as wires when lightning came
and couldn't reach the hard earth.
I took them all in my twenty strides.
They were nothing in the face of you.

I folded up my lives and ran to escape you
but the hard earth opened to swallow my flight,
stretched me taut as wire beneath your lightning.
You greyed my young hair and sold it
to the grasshoppers for their bowstrings. Still
it was not enough. I hid below the grass line,
stayed silent while the rabbits sang,
let the deer dance on me until I bloomed with purple bruises.
When you caught my scent on the wind
I begged the rivers to forget their grudges,
roll themselves over me like lovers in their sleep,
crushing the memories of all I had
before you came. Still you wouldn't give up.
The taste of the twenty lives I could yet live
with you in them sits in my mouth like ash.

Matryoshka Eggs

Tap

the shell of your

tomorrow to reveal

the oval tower nested within,

its curved front door. Knock

with your spoon

and a footman with a smooth, featureless face

will open the door and bow. Behind his yellow

livery a spotlight pencils down from the pinhole

at the top to the pinhole at the bottom, where

the yolk was blown. Membrane curtains flutter

at dome windows; a spiral staircase tongues

the wall. Mount the stairs alone to the

bedroom, where a sloping mantelpiece

bears three portraits: You as a young

woman, you as a mother with a baby

in your lap, you as an old woman

with a white cap and hair. Three

identical smiles mock you

beneath the oval

clock.

The Wolf-Bride

To the thud of drum and the spill of wine
from skins she is carried at midwinter
to her wedding in the wood.

A pretty girl who won't marry is a lit fuse
and the Wolf-King is always hungry;
a deal is struck and no matter how hard

mother sobs, the white dress is stitched tight,
a trousseau packed with meaty bones by whispering
aunts. Strangers offer amulets in waxed paper —

wolf teeth, bone-pearls, carved wings for the afterlife.
She is smiling more than anyone would like.
Better a wolf than a man for a husband, she tells them.

Better a wolf who knows the joy
of loping beneath snow laden trees
than your yoke of slops and pans.

Mother, she says, don't cry, she would rather bear
wolf-cubs; prefers their bark and suckle
to the long cling of a human child.

The drums fall silent as she reaches the clearing
where a seal fat fire burns
under the opal moon; the Wolf-King turns

to behold his reward for eating nothing
but starved beasts when the snows rise like white loaves.
She stares back at his yellow teeth and eyes,

the fur bursting from his necktie,
then at the crown waiting for her on the altar.
She holds out her hand for him to kiss, or bite.

If Leg Wax Were Essential for Tigers

Tiger by tiger the initiation comes
with its gauze strips, its pot of molten
bubble-gum wax, clean purple towels
spread among the bromeliads.

A trained tiger sporting a neat white coat
and painted claws pins down the new girl
with growls, purred cajoling, willingness
to nip a little if the waxee

growls back. Leg by leg she pastes
warm wax onto each stripe
of the youngster's fuzzed pelt,
shushes her roars with small talk

of monkey-hunting holidays as the fur
drowns and peels, follicles harvested
like seeds into the sap of wax.
Strip by strip her colours are claimed,

the embarrassing tufts between each claw.
The trained tiger lotions her crêpe knees,
tells the young tiger she's perfect -
warns that when the hot rain comes,

each drop will land like a hornet
on those bare white legs.

Wheel of Deer

Anxiety is common in prey animals.

Safety is a woodland pool with a flat surface. It is a moment she may witness once in her lifetime and know only by a slight change in her breathing.

Hesitation is a dance of raised hoof and twitching ear. She will be a slave to this choreography all her life; it will haunt the handful of dreams she tumbles into.

Deer do not accept gifts. You may lay before her your life, dipped in honey, and she will not taste it because it bears the unmistakable stench of your fingerprints.

Running is the only prayer she knows. Running is plea. Running is praise. Running is all her body would give up if she were turned inside out by a fox.

Escape is a tunnel entered at birth. Shadows of pursuers stretch, shrink across its walls. She runs, but the circle of freedom dangling ahead never grows any closer.

No one can sing a deer to sleep because a deer can never fully understand what sleep is. Where sleep is the absence of fear, you weight one end of her existence: the total number of eyeballs watching her every movement weights the other. She rests in the fulcrum, vigilant.

Night is an open space which should not be crossed alone. Night is camouflage, night is risk; shelter is the embankment a herd raises against the wind.

Shy curator, 46, seeks love, dancing and romance

she was warm to the touch
from the display lights

heavier than you expected
that perfectly turned body
in its hand stitched dress
the buckles on her tiny boots
so perfect you had to kiss them both

you spoke in the dark
emptied the husk of your heart
into the carved shells of her ears
without ever moving your tongue

danced without music
in a room holding more dust than light
swept her unscuffed feet
across the parquet floor

made her move
the way she must have wanted
after so many years alone
safe with you in the darkness

surely she needed your touch
as you needed hers
the seed pearls of her bodice
rising through their eyelets
like bubbles through champagne

you will never forget tonight
the secret of her crossbar
with its vine of strings
the blossom of her face rising
towards you as forbidden
as it was desired

the weight of her smooth wooden body
resting in your palm like a dead bird

Guidelines for Walking Your Pet Snake Safely

1. Keep your snake in a darkened room for three days prior to walking. When his skin is cool to the touch, pack him in a large suitcase.

2. Zip the suitcase securely. If your snake is particularly devious, add a small padlock.

3. Talk to him about the walk and what treats lay in store while you travel; allow him to anticipate slithering at will amongst the grass and swings.

4. On arrival at your chosen destination, put your ear to the suitcase. If hissing is audible, play soothing music on your pungi before unzipping.

5. Affix your snake's collar and leash. Additional accessories such as cravats or stick-on rhinestones will add wow-factor.

6. Tow your snake lightly across well-mown areas. Playing your pungi, dancing and taking selfies will all help him to recognise you in this new setting.

7. A small but desirable crowd will begin to follow. Keep them entertained with your music and dancing. Pre-rehearsed anecdotes about your snake's lifestyle, such as what style of pyjamas he wears, may add interest.

8. When you are tired of dancing, set up your picnic and feed your snake mouse sandwiches. Ensure thick gloves are worn for this procedure; keep the crowd beyond biting distance.

9. If a crisis occurs, do not panic. Talk to your snake in a calm but stern voice and administer a tranquiliser dart at the first opportunity.

10. Do not allow sentiment for your pet to relax your vigilance. Remember, your snake may not experience love for you in the same way you experience it for him.

Noticing Moths

Night butterflies, we called them, trying to ignore
the alarming bulk of their gibbous bodies in the tent,
antlered heads turning towards the light.
Stay curious, my father said when I jerked back,
away from their glittering in the torchlight;
away from the twitch of wing on canvas. I stayed curious,
kept a moth in a billy can overnight – shuddered
at the thump-thump of wings against metal,
then again in the morning when we unscrewed the can
to find it empty. I stayed curious when years later, descendants
infested my bedroom, filling the air with daughters
thin as splinters, whose bodies burst from their cocoons
full of eggs, ripe for crushing into pearl smears
between thumb and forefinger. *Iridescent is my favourite colour,*
I told my father, wearing the dead moths as eyeshadow.
He didn't seem to notice how I had changed.

Lodging an Informal Complaint

After Melissa Broder

Just once I'd like to walk into my office,
  sit in the swivel chair and have it sprout wings,

    take me and several colleagues for rides
    around the room. As one we'd fly

      out into the corridors then the car park,
      lifting over the Toyotas like a swan.

        I'd like the office mice to leave a tiny gourmet meal
        in my desk drawer, perform cabaret

          on Friday lunchtimes, wear red
          feather boas round their flea-bitten necks.

        The bars on the window could fold themselves
        carefully down, please, and rest their stiff legs;

          let the blossom tree lean in for a chat
          about the small movements outside.

          While the server hummed its one-note tune,
          we'd watch sweet wrappers rolling by

            with microscopic sonnets written on them, dropped
            tissues hitting the pavement, becoming white doves.

RSVP to Robin Goodfellow

Robin Goodfellow, I found your invitation;
one green leaf scratched with your initials

nestled on my step amongst
pizza flyers and pigeon shit.

This year, I have an assignation
with summer. I will come at dawn

when Black Sal is busy
leafing the Jack,

in a green dress with kingcups
studded into my hair. This May Day

we will dance together, Robin Goodfellow.
You can hold me in those sapling arms -

I will lay my garlanded head
on your chest and forget

the siren call of the screen
in my pocket. It's too long

since I smelled your meadow breath.
At sunset I'll head for the suburbs

but before I go, I will light a fire
in your bark encrusted heart

to scorch you all summer long,
Robin Goodfellow, and you will dream of me

when the drummers are gone; when the pumpkins
soften to make a pillow for your russet head

and I am not there to tuck you in.

Have You Seen the Mushroom Man?

The night my blind grandmother
died, I saw him. I walked to the copse,
slipper-clad, to cry without waking
the house and there he was, clambering
from the soil yawning a boneless
yawn, stretching to comb long fingers
through the trees' loose hair.

Something like a smile curved
the hole in his face as he turned
and raised a spindle-finger
to my salt-tracked cheeks,
his breath smelling as she did
those last days: of must and ferment,
threaded with a tang of somewhere
I could never have been

but felt I knew, a place of moonless
root-streets lit only by their own whiteness,
where the old became new,
the place each maggot
longed to return to, pried
every flesh hole to find again.
Staring into his loamy eyes

I pictured her running on wet feet
through streets so soft it would not matter
that she could not see - she could fall and get up
over and over, unhurt, while beetles
marched past on parade and the tight cage
of her bones gradually opened
to let her grow back to the light
as something new.

The Brontë Sisters at Dinner

On Tuesday nights the sisters go to Pizza Express.
Their father is invited, but is usually busy reading the Bible.
Branwell is never invited because of the proximity to wine
but sometimes comes anyway, embarrassing everyone being
drunk on a Tuesday in the only restaurant in Haworth.

Anne is vegan and checks whether the flour
in the ready-made dough is fair trade. The waiting staff
never know but she asks anyway, violet eyes
plucking for guilt, locking their gaze
onto their tiny notebooks.

Emily likes to sit by the window - a small square
of moorland is visible behind the church
if she angles her chair slightly away from her sisters.
Charlotte books the table and mostly pays the bill.
Sometimes she criticises her sisters' menu choices:

The American Hot is too hot for Emily!
Why does Anne worry so much about dairy
when all their neighbours are farmers?
Charlotte always has the same thing.
Together they scribble ideas on the branded napkins,
produce vouchers, leave poems about birds
in the silver dish in place of a tip.

The Woman in the Well

My friend who lives
on the lip of Earth's blowhole,
a mossed funnel of light
and water, spends her days paddling
knee deep in old cloud
fishing with prune fingers
for bone and coin and ore
handing up buckets
of breath-blasted water
and treasures she has found,
down below

while far above
the donkey's overgrown hooves
turn the tread wheel. I sit
patient in the wheelhouse
with my sieve, waiting to see
what the bucket will bring.
Sometimes fresh from a surge
and sometimes stinking,
every tug of the rope
brings new water.

I sift and drink and share
and sometimes get praised
then one day call down to ask
why she continues?

My words bounce around the well
and the donkey skitters,
clatters the wheel.
There is a silence
while she reattaches the pulley
but then she says,

'The people are thirsty'.
(This I know because I drink
more than I pee).
The people are thirsty,
and the well, although old
is a place of certainty,
where bubbles of breath
float up from the sleeping earth
as she dreams her whale dreams.

Keeping My Bones Just So

After dinner I unbutton the onesie
of my skin, peel the muscles
from my bones and puddle them
on the bedroom floor with my tights.

I hook the skeleton on its stand,
brush the dangling joints
then steamclean, rinsing pink juices
from the ivory. Each bone hums

its thanks and gleams. I hum back
with the radio as I click and straighten
the jigsaw; oiling each ball and socket,
the knobbled dinosaur rope of the spine.

I finish with spit, polish
and a chamois leather
then leave the nightlight on for a while
to watch each bone proudly hanging.

I bid them good night, promise breakfast
with milk. To be human is to be hungry
all your life; only the bones are content.
I eat to keep my bones just so.

Meat Dream

I'm thumbnail-tall again tonight and running
down the barrel of a gun, the muzzle
an eye of light watching me in disbelief
that I would even attempt such a feat
and the bullet is gaining, so close I can
hear it whistling, packed tight in its little gold skin,
filling the tunnel like a metal tongue –
but I don't give up, ignore the screams
of my every muscle as I hurl myself towards
that disc of sunlight, the curved edges of safety
I believed would somehow always be mine,
ignoring the drill of the bullet at my back,
keeping my eyes fixed on the circle of air
ahead and survival comes into focus
beyond the tight grip of the gun:
a pair of mild brown eyes with a red light
marking their midpoint, widening in terror
as I thunder closer and prepare to fall.

Song with Feathers

This is a modern sonnet and in saying it is a sonnet,
what I mean is that I have read a thousand sonnets - each a song
of love and hate - and eaten them like dead starlings,
swallowing each bursting heart whole for breakfast,
permitting their fuel of metal and sugar to seep
through my tongue into my blood to feed my brain
writing this sonnet, which is not strictly a sonnet because blood
does not know how to rhyme any more than a bird does,
knows only how to keep flying, keep whispering beneath the hum
of the body - press a knife to your wrist and listen to your blood
sing its echoes of everything you have ever swallowed,
its memories of all the sterile chopped up birds you ever fed it,
then think how hungry it must be for something real,
something raw, something with feathers - something like a sonnet.

Bright Carver

After Gormenghast

We the cooks of wood and colour
we make them we do it
proud duty for Earl Groan
no trees left now we go far
cross the sea of mud and stump
cut cut cut for the dryad
cut cut cut for the dragon's head
big trees tight with futures
we hush their whispering
feel in knot and bole
a tiger here a griffin there
find wildflowers and beetles
pound them into bright
make emerald horse, piebald shark
spray with foxglove
stroke on bluebell belly
with a horsetail brush
haul carvings like fried rats
from the hot oil of ideas
I'll be my father's son
lick the splinters with a clean tongue
it don't matter no one sees them
the Earl shall know the worth of my hand

Acknowledgements

I would like to thank my parents, Nick and my endlessly supportive Buddhist friends for their encouragement in the process of creating these poems. Further thanks are owed to my Arvon pals and fellow poets at the Poetry School, the Faber Academy, SKEGS and Manor Farm Poets for their guidance and fine-tuning.

Lastly, I owe a profound debt of gratitude to my Buddhist mentor, Daisaku Ikeda, for always believing in my potential and insisting I do the same.

Poems in this pamphlet have previously appeared in *Islands Are But Mountains,* an anthology of contemporary British poetry by Platypus Press, the *Elements* anthology published by Fawn Press, *The North, Tears in the Fence, Lighthouse Journal, Shearsman, Fenland Poetry Journal, Prole* and *Under the Radar. Families Can Only be Grown on Arable Land* was shortlisted for the Café Writers Prize and longlisted for the National Poetry Competition in 2021; *An ill wind* was published by the Poetry School as part of the Primers shortlist in 2019.

Quotes have been taken from Sharon Olds, Shannon Wiltsey Stirman, Robert Lowell and Anne Sexton.